CRYSTAL COAST COOKERY

J. HILL

Old School Recipes from
North Carolina Coast Home Cooks

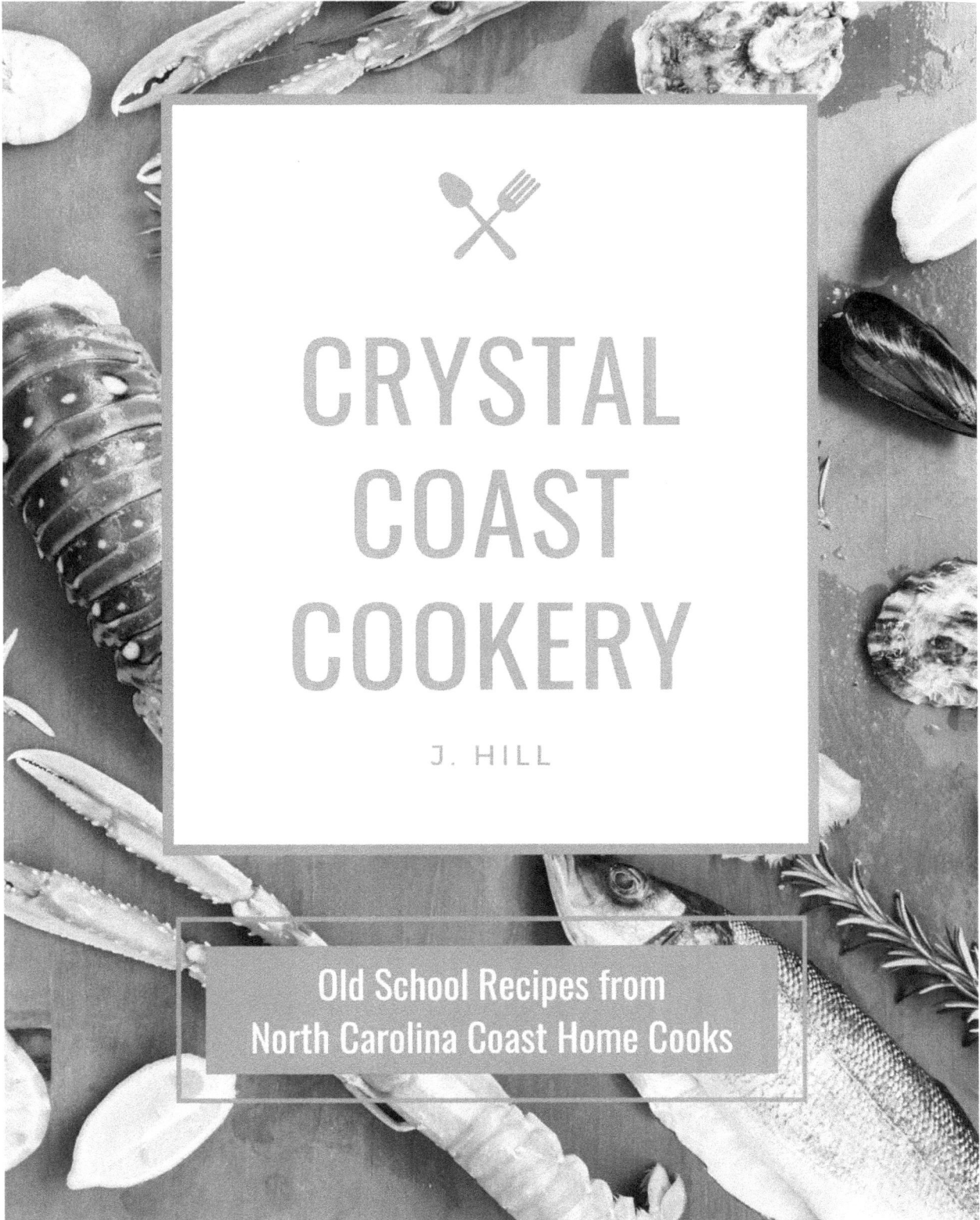

Crystal Coast Cookery

OLD SCHOOL RECIPES FROM
NORTH CAROLINA COAST HOME COOKS

Introduction

From church fundraisers to Sunday dinner tables, these are recipes that have been passed down from generation to generation, swapped among friends, and shared, hastily written, on the corners of receipts, the backs of can labels, and the corners of disused almanacs.

These are the recipes of the people, developed in their own kitchens, for their own families, to their own tastes.

You are welcomed with abundant Southern Hospitality to share in this "mess of good eatin'."

The majority of these recipes are from the 1950s through the 1970s from sources throughout the coastal and Outer Banks communities of North Carolina.
Where original ingredients are no longer available, substitutions have been suggested.

Hors d'oeuvres, Pickles & Casseroles

REFRIGERATOR PICKLES

3 C VINEGAR (WHITE OR APPLE CIDER)   3 C WATER
3 TBSP PICKLING SALT*   2 TBSP SUGAR
2 BAY LEAF   1 TBSP WHOLE PEPPERCORNS
2 TBSP DILL, CELERY SEED, OR
MUSTARD SEED

FOR SWEET PICKLES SUSBTITUTE:
3 TBSP PICKLING SALT*   1 1/2 C SUGAR

*Note: You can substitute Kosher Salt for Pickling Salt.

Bring vinegar, water, salt, sugar, and seasonings to a boil to make brine. Set aside to cool. Slice cucumbers – peel, if desired. Place sliced cucumbers into mason jars and pour cooled brine over, leave ¼ inch headspace. Best after 1 to 2 day in refrigerator, good for up to two weeks.

PICKLED ONIONS

2 C VINEGAR (WHITE OR APPLE CIDER)   2 C WATER
2 TBSP PICKLING SALT*   4 TBSP SUGAR
2 BAY LEAF   1 TBSP WHOLE PEPPERCORNS
3 MEDIUM ONIONS, THINLY SLICED

*Note: You can substitute Kosher Salt for Pickling Salt.

Bring vinegar, water, salt, sugar, and seasonings to a boil to make brine. Set aside to cool. Pack thinly sliced onions into jar(s). Pour cooled brine over, leave ¼ inch headspace.

SQUASH CASSEROLE

2 C COOKED SQUASH
¾ STICK BUTTER
2 EGGS
1 TSP SALT
½ TSP PEPPER

1 C CHOPPED ONION
1 C EVAPORATED MILK
2 C CRACKER CRUMBS
I C GRATED CHEESE

Mash cooked squash. Add other ingredients and mix well. Pout into greased baking dish and bake at 375 degrees for 40 minutes. Top with extra cheese if desired and brown.

CREAMY BROCCOLI & RICE CASSEROLE

1 STICK MARGARINE (OR BUTTER)
¾ C CHOPPED ONION
¾ C CHOPPED CELERY
1 CAN CREAM OF CHICKEN SOUP
2 C WARM WATER

1 CAN CREAM OF MUSHROOM SOUP
2 PACKS FROZEN BROCCOLI, COOKED
2 C MINUTE RICE
1 LARGE JAR CHEEZ WHIZ*

* Large Cheez Wiz is approx.. 15 oz. Can substitute 2 C melted Velveeta or similar.

Combine all ingredients and mix well. Bake in large greased casserole dish for 1 hour at 325 degrees.

CHEESY POTATO CASSEROLE

4 LARGE POTATOES
1 CAN CHEDDR CHEESE SOUP
GRATED CHEESE, OPTIONAL

3 MEDIUM ONIONS
BUTTER

Peel and thinly slice potatoes. Thinly slice onions. In a buttered baking dish, put layer of potatoes followed by layers of onion until dish is 2/3 full. Add can of cheese soup evenly over potatoes and onions. Bake at 400 degrees for approx. 30 minutes or until potatoes are fork tender. Add grated cheese and brown, if desired.

SEAFOOD CASSEROLE

1 LB CRABMEAT	1 C MAYONNAISE
1 LB SHRIMP, BOILED	1 TBSP WORCESTERSHIRE SAUCE
½ C GREEN PEPPER, DICED	½ TSP SALT
1 ½ C CELERY, DICED	¼ TSP PEPPER
¼ C ONION, DICED	2 C POTATO CHIPS, CRUSHED
PAPRIKA	

Mix all but chips and paprika and put in a greased casserole dish. Cover with crushed chips and sprinkle with paprika. Bake in 400 degree oven for 20 to 25 minutes. Cracker crumbs can be used instead of chips.

SAVOURY RICE

1 STICK MARGARINE (OR BUTTER)	1 CAN BEEF CONSOMME
3 C WHITE RICE, UNCOOKED	1 ½ C WATER
2 CANS BEEF BROTH	ONION FLAKES
2 BOUILLON CUBES	GARLIC SALT

Mix all ingredients. Cover and bake 60 minutes at 350 degrees, making sure to stir thoroughly at the 30 minute mark.

CHEESY BROCCOLI BACON CASSEROLE

2 PKG FROZEN BROCCOLI	2 C MILK
4 SLICES COOKED BACON, CRUMBLED	¾ C SHREDDED CHEESE
2 TSP BUTTER	1 C BUTTERED BREAD CRUMBS
2 TSP FLOUR	SALT AND PEPPER TO TASTE

Cook broccoli slightly, drain, place in casserole dish. Make a cream sauce of butter, flour, milk and cheese. Pour broccoli in dish. Add crumbled bacon. Top with buttered bread crumbs. Bake at 375 degrees for about 25 minutes.

CHEESE DIP

8 OZ CREAM CHEESE   1 SMALL JAR CHERRIES
1 SMALL CAN CRUSHED PINEAPPLE   I C CHOPPED NUTS

Combine all ingredients and chill. If too thick, add a little pineapple juice. Great with crackers or chips.

CHEESE-PECAN ROLLS

1 LB VELVEETA   ½ C PECANS, FINELY CHOPPED
1 TSP GARLIC SALT OR POWDER   1 TBSP CHILI POWDER

Mix together and roll in chili powder. Chill and slice off as needed. Best on buttery crackers.

NIBBLE BAIT

1 SMALL BOX PRETZEL STICKS   ½ C BUTTER OR MARGARINE
2 C CHEERIOS   1 TSP GARLIC SALT
2 C RICE CHEX   1 TSP CELERY SALT
2 C MIXED NUTS   1 TSP ONION SALT
2 C BITE-SZE SHREDDED WHEAT
BISCUITS

Combine pretzel sticks, cereals, and nuts in a shallow baking dish. Put butter in small pieces on top of cereal, then sprinkle on the garlic, onion, and celery salt. Bake in slow over 250 degrees for 30 minutes, stirring often. Serve hot or cold.

CORN PUFFS

1 EGG   1 ½ TBSP SUGAR
1 SMALL CAN CREAMED CORN   ½ TSP BAKING POWDER
SALT AND PEPPER TO TASTE

Beat egg. Add corn, sugar, baking powder, and salt. Thicken with flour. Drop into hot, deep oil and cook until done.

CHICKEN AND RICE CASSEROLE

10.5 OZ CONDENSED MUSHROOM SOUP
¾ C MILK
1 TBSP ONION, FINELY CHOPPED
1 TBSP CHOPPED PARSELY

1 C HERBED STUFFING MIX
¼ C MELTED BUTTER OR MARGARINE
3 C COOKED RICE
2 LB CHICKEN PARTS

Mix 1/3 C soup, ¼ C milk, onion, and parsley. Dip chicken in soup mixture; then roll in stuffing, do all pieces of chicken and lay them aside. Mix together the remainder of the soup and the soup dipping mixture with the rice and place in casserole dish. Places the chicken over this. Bake at 400 degrees for 1 hour or until done.

Variation: Instead of herbed stuffing, use 1 C fine dry bread crumbs, ½ TSP Poultry Seasoning, and ½ TSP Salt.

BAKED BEANS

1 LARGE CAN BAKED BEANS
1 C LIGHT BROWN SUGAR, PACKED
½ C KARO SYRUP
SALT AND PEPPER TO TASTE

1 SMALL ONION, CHOPPED
4 SLICES BACON
½ BOTTLE KETCHUP

Empty beans in casserole or baking dish. Mix all ingredients into beans, place bacon slices on top. Bake in 300 degrees over or bacon has cooked thoroughly and beans have browned on edges.

ESCALLOPED POTATOES

5 OR 6 MEDIUM POTATOES
3 TBSP FLOUR
1 TSP SALT

1 ½ C MILK
2 TBSP BUTTER

Wash potatoes, pare and slice thin. Combine flour and salt. Arrange 1/3 of the potatoes in bottom of a greased baking dish; sprinkle with 1/3 of the flour and salt mixture. Repeat. Pour on scalded milk and dot with butter. Cover and bake in a medium oven (375 degrees) for 45 minutes, then uncover and bake for 15 to 20 minutes longer, or until potatoes are tender.

Salads, Soups & Vegetables

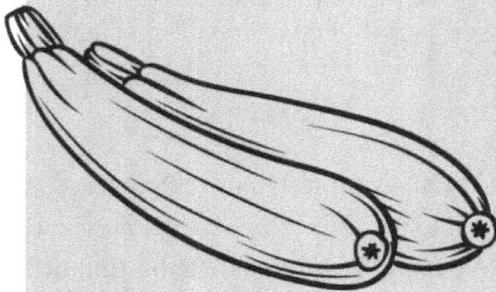

AUNT NELL'S LAZY WOMAN SLAW

1 LARGE HEAD CABBAGE
1 TBSP SALT
2 RED PEPPERS
2 GREEN PEPPERS
2 C SUGAR

1 C WHITE VINEGAR
½ C WATER
½ BUNCH CELERY
½ TBSP CELERY SEED
½ TBSP MUSTARD SEED

Shred cabbage, add salt. Let stand for one hour, then squeeze out liquid. Add peppers, celery, mustard seed, and celery seed. Boils sugar, vinegar, and water. When cool pour over the above mixture. Keep in refrigerator. Let it set for a few hours before serving.

Note: Carrots may be used instead of Peppers if desired.

GILIKIN CLAM CHOWDER

1 QT CLAMS
2 C DICED WHITE POTATOES
2 SMALL ONIONS, FINE CHOP
2 SLICES FAT BACK

1 C CORN MEAL
SALT TO TASTE
BLACK PEPPER TO TASTE

Chop clams and cook in large Dutch oven. Add 1 QT water to clams and bring to boil. Reduce heat to medium boil and add onions, salt, and pepper. Fry fat back and brown 1/3 C flour in rendered fat. Add clams, onions. Cook on low heat for 30 minutes. Add potatoes. When all ingredients boil, cook for 30 minutes longer. Add corn meal dumplings and cook on low heat for 1 hour longer. Add water if needed while cooking.

To make dumplings: Stir corn meal with warm water, adding dash of salt. Make a soft mixture and pat out dumplings. Place around side of pot while cooking.

CORE SOUND OYSTER STEW

¼ LB SALT PORK
2 QT OYSTERS
1 C WATER

½ TSP BLACK PEPPER
SALT (TO TASTE)
CORN MEAL DUMPLINGS (SEE BELOW)

Cut pork into small cubes and fry until crispy and lightly browned. Add oysters, water, and black pepper. Salt to taste. Heat and serve. If adding corn meal dumplings, cover and simmer 20 to 25 minutes or until dumplings are done to preference.

CORN MEAL DUMPLINGS

1 ½ C CORNMEAL

1 MEDIUM ONION, MINCED OR 1 TBSP
ONION POWDER

½ TSP SALT

1 C ALL-PURPOSE FLOUR

½ C MILK, OR WATER

¼ TSP PEPPER

Combine the cornmeal with flour. Add onion/powder, salt and pepper. Add ½ liquid of choice to dry ingredients until just combined in a thick batter. Use two teaspoons to form dumplings and drop in cooking liquid/stew.

ELECTION NIGHT STEW

1 LB GROUND BEEF

1 LARGE ONIONS, CHOPPED

2 TBSP OIL

1 C PRE-COOKED RICE

1 C BOILING WATER

1 CAN CRUSHED TOMATOES

1 CAN KIDNEY BEANS

1 ¼ TSP SALT

½ TSP PEPPER

½ TSP WORCESTERSHIRE SAUCE

1 TSP CHILI POWDER

Brown meat and onion in oil, add rice and cook until golden. Stir in remaining ingredients. Simmer for 15 minutes.

POTATO SALAD

4 C POTATOES, DICED

½ C ONION, DICED

3 OR 4 HARD BOILED EGGS, CHOPPED

½ C PICKLES, DICED

2 TSP SALT

½ C MAYONNAISE

3 TBSP MUSTARD

PAPRIKA

Peel and dice potatoes. Cook in salted water until fork tender. In mixing bowl, place cooled cooked potatoes. Mix in diced onions, chopped eggs, pickles, and add salt and pepper to taste. Stir in mayonnaise and mustard until well mixed. When serving, sprinkle with paprika.

BEAN SALAD

1 CAN RED KIDNEY BEANS
1 CAN CUT GREEN BEANS
1 CAN CUT WAX BEANS*
1 TSP SALT
½ VEGETABLE OIL

1 MED ONION, DICED OR THIN SLICED
¾ C SUGAR
2/3 C VINEGAR
½ TSP PEPPER

*Note: Wax beans substitutes: garbanzo/chickpeas, thin asparagus

*Note: Olive, avocado, or any salad oil can be used

Drains and rinse all beans thoroughly. In large bowl combine beans and onions. Dissolve sugar in vinegar and whisk with oil, add salt and pepper. Pour over beans and onions, and toss. Marinate overnight in the refrigerator.

SHRIMP SALAD

2 LBS SHRIMP
2 SWEET PEPPERS, DICED
1 LARGE ONION, DICED
SALT AND PEPPER TO TASTE

6 C DICED IRISH POTATOES*
3 HARD BOILED EGGS
3 TBSP SALAD DRESSING

*Note: Can substitute small red potatoes

Peel and clean shrimp. Put shrimp in a boiler and cover with salty water. Cook 20 minutes. Drain shrimp and cut in half. Cook diced potatoes in boiling water until soft. Drain. Combine shrimp, potatoes, eggs, onion, pepper in a large bowl. Add salt, pepper, and salad dressing. Mix all ingredients well.

SHRIMP AND MACARONI SALAD

1 LB BOILED SHRIMP, CHOPPED
2 C ELBOW MACARONI, COOKED
½ C CELERY, FINELY CHOPPED
¼ C SWEET PICKLES, CHOPPED
½ C SALAD DRESSING

1 TBSP LEMON JUICE
1 TBSP GRATED ONION
1 TBSP SALT
1 TBSP PEPPER
2 BOILED EGGS

Mix all ingredients together in a bowl and chill. Serve on lettuce with slices of boiled eggs and tomato wedges.

CHICKEN SALAD SUPREME

4 COOKED CHICKEN BREASTS, DICED
1 CPICKLE RELISH
¾ C MAYONNAISE

1 SMALL BOTTLE CHOPPED CHERRIES
¼ C CHOPPED PECANS

Combine all ingredients and chill.

STUFFED PEPPERS

6 SWEET PEPPERS
2 ½ LBS GROUND BEEF
2 SMALL ONIONS, DICED
1 LARGE POTATO, DICED

1 PACK HAMBURGER SEASONING*
1 TSP SALT
½ TSP BLACK PEPPER
1 CAN TOMATO SAUCE

* Note: Also known as Grill Seasoning

Core the peppers. Wash and let drain. In large mixing bowl mix beef, salt, pepper, and hamburger/grill seasoning. Then add potato and onion. Stuff mixture into peppers. Preheat oven to 375 degrees. Put peppers in loaf pan. Cover pan with aluminium foil. Let cook one hour. Take foil off and put tomato sauce on top of peppers and let brown.

CANDIED SWEET POTATOES

6 SWEET POTATOES
1 C BROWN SUGAR
¼ C WATER

¼ C MARGARINE (OR BUTTER)
½ TSP SALT

Cook sweet potatoes until tender, drain and peel. Make a syrup of remaining ingredients and boil 5 minutes. Slice potatoes lengthwise and place in a shallow baking dish. Pour syrup over potatoes and bake in 350 degree oven about 25 minutes. Potatoes may be basted with syrup during baking if desired.

YUMMY YAMS

4 LARGE YAMS

2/3 TO ¾ C SUGAR (WHITE OR BROWN)

PINCH OF SALT

1/3 C THICK CREAM OR EVAP MILK

CINNAMON, IF DESIRED

Butter a 13 x 9 x 2 inch baking dish. Peel yams and cut into strips like French Fries. Add sugar, salt, and cream/evaporated milk. (Amount of sugar will vary according to size of yams.) Bake at 450 degrees for about 45 minutes. Cover with aluminium foil to prevent drying out while baking. Grated cheese or marshmallows may be used as topping.

Notes_____

Meat, Fish & Poultry

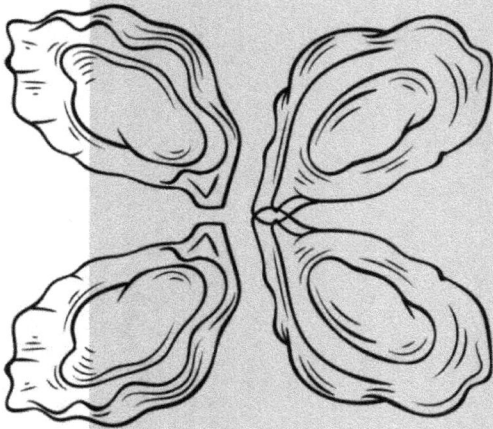

CRAB CAKES

1 LB CRAB MEAT
4 TBSP MELTED BUTTER
½ TSP SALT
½ TSP PEPPER

PINCH OF CAYENNE PEPPER
2 EGGS
2 C BREAD CRUMBS
1 TBSP WATER

In a bowl add crabmeat and seasonings. Add eggs, well beaten, until mixture is firm enough to mould into small cakes, reserving about 1/3 of eggs. Add 1 TBSP water to reserved beaten eggs. Dip formed cakes into egg then roll in bread crumbs until covered. Sauté in heavy frying pan with oil of choice until browned. If deep frying, hold oil at 380 degrees.

THE SANITARY'S SHRIMP CREOLE STYLE

1 ½ LB SHRIMP
¼ C ONION
¼ C GREEN PEPPER
1 CLOVE GARLIC, MINCED
¼ C BUTTER
3 TBSP FLOUR

1 TSP CHILI POWDER
1 TSP SALT
2 C TOMATOES
1/8 TSP PEPPER
2 C RICE

Boil and drain shrimp. Combine all other ingredients except rice over medium heat and cook until tender. Serve over steamed rice.

DEEP FRIED SHRIMP

1 LB SHRIMP
½ TSP SALT
1 C WATER

2 TBSP BAKING POWDER
1 EGG
1 C FLOUR

Combine all ingredients except shrimp and blend into batter. Dip shrimp into batter then into hot grease/fat and cook until golden brown. Delicious accompanied with hushpuppies and slaw.

DEEP FRIED CLAMS

1 QT CLAMS
1 EGG, BEATEN
1 TBSP MILK

1 TSP SALT
½ TSP PEPPER
1 C DRY BREAD OR CRACKER CRUMBS

Drain clams. Combine eggs, milk, and seasonings. Dip clams in egg mixture and roll in crumbs. Fry in a basket in deep fat for 2 or 3 minutes or until brown. Serve plain or with a sauce.

DEVILED CLAMS

1 DOZEN OR 1 CAN MINCED CLAMS
3 HARD BOILED EGGS, MINCED
1 SMALL, MINCED
BUTTER

3 TBSP CORNFLAKE, CRUSHED
SALT AND PEPPER TO TASTE
½ C MAYONNAISE

Mix all ingredients with mayonnaise. Pack in shells and cover with cornflake crumbs. Put ½ pat butter on top. Bake in 350 degrees for about 25 or 30 minutes.

CHARCOAL BROILED MULLETS

6 JUMPING MULLETS
1 MEDIUM ONION, FINELY DICED
1 C KETCHUP
2 TBSP VINEGAR

½ LEMON (JUICED)
HOT SAUCE TO TASTE
I TSP MUSTARD

Clean fish, remove head and backbone. Leave scaled on fish. Wash fish and cover with salt. Remove salt from fish after 45 minutes. Drain well and pat dry. Place fish on charcoal grill, scales down. Spread sauce* mixtures over fish. Cook slowly until fish begins to bubble. Turn fish and cook slowly for five minutes longer. Remove and eat meat from shell formed by skin and scaled.

Sauce: Combine Ketchup, Onion, Mustard, and Vinegar. Add hot sauce to taste.

SHE-CRAB SOUP

1 LB CRAB MEAT, PICKED
¼ C MINCED ONION
3 C STOCK OR WATER
SEASONINGS:
½ TSP WORCHESTERSHIRE SAUCE
¼ TSP CAYENNE PEPPER
¼ TSP PAPRIKA
½ TSP BLACK PEPPER

¼ C BUTTER
¼ C FLOUR
2 C HEAVY CREAM OR HALF N HALF

1 TSP SALT
½ TSP CELERY SEED
¼ MUSTARD
½ TSP NUTMEG

Melt butter on medium heat and cook onion until soft, translucent but not brown. Add flour to make a roux and cook out flour for a couple of minutes until like a smooth. Add stock (or water), stirring well, and reduce to low until thickened, stirring occasionally. To room temperature cream (or half-n-half) add a slight bit of roux to temper cream. Add cream to stock mixture and bring to a boil. Then reduce to low and add all seasonings, stirring to combine. Add crab meat, reserving some for garnish. Simmer all for five minutes. Sprinkle reserved crab meat over individual bowls when serving or atop serving bowl. Delicious with a spritz of lemon or splash of sherry vinegar over finished bowl.

ALMOST AS GOOD AS EL'S SHRIMP BURGER

1 ½ LB SHRIMP
SALT
COLESLAW
4 C FRYING OIL

2 ½ C CRACKER MEAL (SEE BELOW)
SOFT WHITE HAMBURGER BUNS
KETCHUP

Get good shrimp. Clean and devein shrimp. Sprinkle shrimp with salt and let sit. Roll shrimp in cracker meal and deep fry until golden brown. Serve on soft white buns, with lots and slaw and ketchup on top. You don't have to eat them with hushpuppies, but why wouldn't you.

HOMEMADE CRACKER MEAL

1 14 OZ BOX SALTINE CRACKERS
SALT

½ TSP PAPRIKA
PEPPER

Pulse all ingredients until a fine meal. Alternately, crush crackers in a plastic bag until crumbs and add seasonings to crumbs.

SWEDISH STYLE SPARERIBS

2 LBS SPARERIBS	1 TBSP ALLSPICE
¼ TSP PEPPER	¼ C BUTTER OR MARGARINE
1 TSP SUGAR	1 BOUILLON CUBE
1 TBSP SALT	1 C HOT WATER

Cut spareribs into 2 or 3 rib pieces. Sprinkle with combined dry ingredients. Sauté ribs in hot butter until brown on both sides. Melt bouillon cube in hot water and add to ribs. Simmer, covered, until fork tender – around 90 minutes.

FLUFFY MEAT LOAF

1 LB GROUND BEEF OR VEAL	¼ C MINCED ONION
½ LEAN GROUND PORK	1 ¼ TSP SALT
3 SLICE SOFT BREAD, TORN*	1 C MILK*
1 EGG, BEATEN	¼ TSP PEPPER
¼ TSP SAGE	¼ TSP DRY MUSTARD
¼ TSP GARLIC SALT	1 TBSP WORCESTERSHIRE SAUCE
¼ TSP CELERY SALT	

* Can substitute 1 ¼ C MILK + 1 C BREAD CRUMBS for Sliced Bread + Milk

Heat oven to 350 degrees. Mix all ingredients thoroughly. For better browning, shape into loaf on a shallow baking pain. Bake 90 minutes or until done. Serve hot or cold.

SWISS STEAK

1 LB BEEF, ROUND CUT	3 TBSP CHOPPED GREEN PEPPER
1 MEDIUM ONION, SLICED	1 SMALL CAN TOMATO SAUCE
3 TBSP COOKING OIL	1 ½ TSP SALT
1 C WATER	¼ TSP PEPPER
1 ½ C FLOUR	1 TBSP WORCESTERSHIRE SAUCE

* Can substitute 1 ¼ C MILK + 1 C BREAD CRUMBS for Sliced Bread + Milk

Coat flour, salt, and pepper into steak. Sear on both sides in oil. After searing put onion and pepper and Worcestershire sauce on top of steak Add water. Then cook slowly for 60 to 90 minutes. When half done, add tomato sauce.

NEW ENGLAND BOILED DINNER

4 LBS CORNED BRISKET OF BEEF
8 SMALL ONIONS
8 WHOLE CARROTS

4 POTATOES, QUARTERED
2 TURNIPS, CUBED
1 GREEN CABBAGE, CUT IN WEDGES

Place meat in heavy pot. Cover with hot water. Cover tightly and simmer about 3 hours. Skim of excess fat and add onions, carrots, potatoes, and turnips. Cover and cook 20 minutes. Add cabbage and continue to cook for 10 to 15 minutes or until vegetables tender.

COUNTRY BURGERS

1 LB GROUND BEEF
1 CAN CHICKEN GUMBO SOUP

1 BELL PEPPER
1 SMALL ONION

Dice onion, pepper and cook together until browned. Add the ground beef and brown. Add gumbo soup and season with salt and pepper to taste. Serve on hamburger buns.

HAMBURGER PIE

1 LB GROUND BEEF
1 ONION
1/C MILK
SALT AND PEPPER TO TASTE

1 CAN TOMATO SOUP
5 POTATOES
1 CAN GREEN BEANS

Cook onion and add meat to brown. Add beans and soup. Pour into baking dish. Cream potatoes and spoon over meat. Bake at 350 degrees for 30 minutes until golden brown on top.

ITALIAN BAKED CHICKEN

3 LBS FRYER, CUT UP
3 MEDIUM ONIONS

3 C ITALIAN BREADCRUMBS
MILK

Dip chicken pieces in milk and then roll in breadcrumbs. Place in baking dish. Thinly slice the onions and layer over the chicken. Cover and bake at 350 degrees for 45 minutes or until chicken is done. Uncover and bake for 15 to 20 more until chicken and onions are crispy.

SKILLET MACARONI AND BEEF

1 ½ LB GROUND BEEF
2 TBSP VEGETABLE OIL
½ LB UNCOOKED ELBOW MACARONI
½ C CHOPPED ONION
½ C CHOPPED GREEN PEPPER
2 8 OZ CANS TOMATO SAUCE (16 OZ)

1 C WATER (MORE AS NEEDED)
1 TSP SALT
¼ TSP PEPPER
1 ½ WORCESTERSHIRE SAUCE
½ TSP GARLIC POWDER

Lightly brown beef in skillet with oil. Add remaining ingredients. Cook 25 minutes or until macaroni is cooked.

SUMMER PEAS AND CHICKEN IN SOUR CREAM

6 TBSP BUTTER OR MARGARINE
1 2 ½ LB FRYING CHICKEN OR BREASTS
1 LB SMALL POTATOES
2 TBSP FRESH LEMON JUICE
3 SCALLIONS/GREEN ONION, SLICED
¼ TSP SALT
ADDITIONAL PARSLEY FOR GARNISH

1 LB FRESH GREEN PEAS
1 10 OZ PKG FROZEN PEAS
1/C CHOPPED FRESH PARSLEY
1 C SOUR CREAM
½ TSP DRIED THYME
1/8 TSP PEPPER PLUS MORE

Melt butter in large skillet. Add chicken and potatoes and brown slowly on all sides; season with salt and pepper. (Be generous with pepper.) Sprinkle chicken with lemon juice; reduce heat. Cover pan and simmer for 30 minutes. Add green onion to butter in bottom of skillet; sprinkle peas and parsley over chicken and potatoes; cover again and simmer for 10 minutes more or until chicken and potatoes are tender. Remove chicken and vegetables to platter; keep warm. Remove skillet from heat. Add sour cream, thyme, ¼ tsp salt and 1/8 tsp pepper, stir to mix well and to loosen pan drippings. Pour over chicken or peas as sauce. Garnish with additional parsley; serve immediately.

BARBECUED CHICKEN

3 LB FRYER, CUT UP
3 TBSP FLOUR
SAUCE:
1 MEDIUM BOTTLE OF KETCHUP
¼ C VINEGAR
1 TSP HOT SAUCE

1 STICK MARGARINE OR BUTTER
SALT

1 MEDIUM ONION
1/3 C SUGAR
½ PKG ITALIAN SALAD MIX

Wash, salt, and flour chicken. Arrange in baking pan in which margarine has been melted. Mix sauce ingredients in saucepan and bring mixture to a boil and pour over chicken. Cover and bake at 350 degrees for 45 minutes to an hour. Remove cover for last 20 minutes to brown. Flour from chicken thickens the sauce as cooks. Serve hot.

*Notes*_____

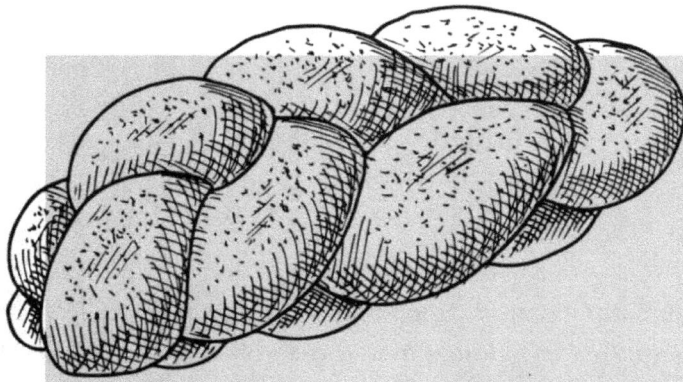

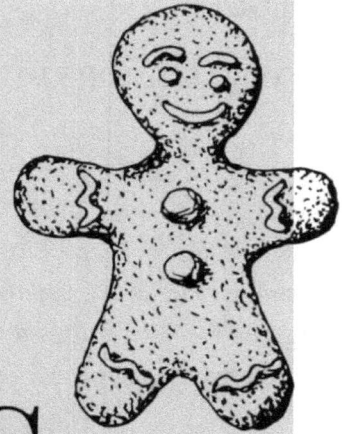

Breads, Rolls & Cookies

LIGHT ROLLS

½ PKG YEAST
1 C WARM WATER
1 TBSP SUGAR (TO MIX INTO YEAST)

3 C FLOUR
3 TBSP SUGAR
1 TBSP SALT

Mix yeast, warm water. Stir and add 1 TBSP sugar. Let stand about 10 minutes for yeast to bloom and soften. Sift dry ingredients together and add liquid to this. Knead into a medium firm dough adding more flour or liquid if necessary. Let dough rise until doubled. Fold or knew down and let rise ¾ as much as the first time. Fold down again and shape as you wish. Let rise in greased pan until doubled. Bake about 20 minutes in medium hot over (400 degrees).

TARHEEL HUSH PUPPIES

1 LB FINE CORN MEAL
1 EGG
1 TBSP SALT

1 TBSP SUGAR
PINCH OF BAKING SODA
1 C BUTTERMILK

Stir, adding water, to thick consistency. Drop in deep fat to fry. Cook in temperature of 375 degrees.

MRS IVA'S CORN BREAD

1 C CORN MEAL
½ C FLOUR
2 TSP BAKING POWDER
1 TBSP SUGAR

½ TSP SALT
1 EGG
1 TBSP OIL
1 C MILK

Heat oven to 425 degrees. Pour about 3 TBSP shortening in pan. Put in oven and heat while mixing batter. Mix all dry ingredients in a bowl. Beat in egg and oil, then add milk all at once. Mix well, then pour into hot pan. Bake about 25 minutes or until brown.

SWEET POTATO BISCUITS

1 C ALL PURPOSE FLOUR
3 TBSP BAKING POWDER
½ TSP SALT

3 TBSP LARD/SHORTENING
1 C COOKED, MASHED SWEET POTATO
¼ C MILK

Sift together the dry ingredients. Cut in the fat. Add the mashed sweet potatoes and mix well. Add gradually enough milk to make a soft dough. Kneed a few strokes. Roll dough 1/3 inch thick. Cut in rounds and place on baking sheet. Bake in 450 degree oven 12 to 15 minutes.

DATE NUT BARS

1 C PLAIN FLOUR
½ TSP BAKING POWDER
½ TSP SALT
½ C SHORTENING OR BUTTER
½ C SUGAR

2 EGGS
1 TSP VANILLA
1 PKG DATES
1 C NUTS

Beat eggs until foamy. Beat in sugar and vanilla. Sift dry ingredients and stir into other ingredients. Mix in nuts and dates (chopped in you like). Spread in greased pan. Bake in a moderately slow oven, 325 degrees, for 25 to 35 minutes. Cut in squares while warm. Cool, then remove from pan.

DATE STICKS

2 C SUGAR
4 TBSP BUTTER
4 EGGS
2 TBSP HOT WATER
CONFECTIONERS SUGAR FOR GARNISH

2 TSP BAKING POWDER
1 C CHOPPED NUTES
2 LBS DATES, CUT FINE
½ TSP SALT

Mix together and spread in well-greased baking pan and bake at 325 degrees for 25 minutes. Sprinkle with confectioners' sugar and cut into 1 inch long pieces. Remove from pan and place on wire rack to cool.

CINNAMON ROLLS

3 C LUKEWARM BUTTERMILK
1 PKG YEAST
2 C FLOUR
½ C SUGAR + 1 C SUGAR
1 C RAISINS
2 TBSP CINNAMON

1 TSP SALT
1 TSP BAKING SODA
1 EGG
½ C SHORTENING
1 STICK MARGARINE, SOFTENED

TOPPING:

1 LB CONFECTIONERS SUGAR
1 EGG WHITE

1/8 TSP SALT
4 TBSP EVAPORATED MILK

Add warm water to yeast, and let stand until dissolved. Mix ingredients (incl ½ cup sugar) together. Let dough stand in warm place until it doubles in bulk. Knew dough for several minutes and roll dough out until ¼ inch thick. Spread with soft margarine and sprinkle with 1 cup sugar mixed with 2 TBSP cinnamon. Roll dough as you would for a jelly roll. Cut into 1 inch pieces and place in well-greased pan. Let rise until doubled in bulk. Bake at 425 degrees until lightly brown. Spread each roll with topping.

Topping: Cream together confectioners' sugar, 1/8 TSP salt, egg white, and evaporated milk. Mix well until spreads easily.

CHEESE COATED DATES

½ LB SHARP CHEDDAR, GRATED
1 STICK BUTTER OR MARGARINE
1 ½ C PLAIN FLOUR
DASH OF SALT

DASH OF CAYENNE PEPPER
1 LB DATES
NUTS

Mix cheese, butter, flour, and salt together to form dough. Pinch off dough, put in a date that has been stuffed with a nut and fold in hand until date is covered. Put on cookie sheet and bake at 300 degrees for 30 minutes or until brown as desired.

DARLENE'S CHEWY BROWNIES

2 SQ (2 OZ) UNSWEETENED CHOCOLATE

1 C SUGAR

2 TBSP BUTTER

1 EGG

1 EGG

1 TSP VANILLA

1 C SIFTED FLOUR

1 TSP BAKING POWDER

½ C EVAPORATED MILK

1 C CHOPPED NUTS

Melt chocolate in pan. Put sugar, butter, egg, and vanilla in bowl and mix. Pour the melted chocolate into the sugar, butter mixture. Sift flour with baking powder. Stir half the flour mixtures into the butter. Add milk. Stir batter until smooth. Add rest of flour and chopped nuts. Pour into buttered 9 inch square pan. Bake about 30 minutes at 350 degrees.

CHOCOLATE BROWNIES

¾ C SIFTED FLOUR

1 C SUGAR

5 TBSP COCOA POWDER

½ TSP SALT

½ C SHORTENING, SOFTENED

2 EGGS, UNBEATEN

1 TSP VANILLA

½ C CHOPPED NUTES

Have all ingredients at room temperature. Place all ingredients in large bowl. Beat at medium speed for about 3 minutes. Preheat oven to 350 degrees, grease bottom of 8 inch square pan. Bake for 30 minutes.

BOILED COOKIES

2 C SUGAR

½ C MILK

¼ LB MARGARINE OR BUTTER

4 TBSP COCOA POWDER

2 1/3 C QUICK COOKING OATS

¼ C CHOPPED NUTS

2 TSP VANILLA

½ C PEANUT BUTTER

Combine sugar, margarine/butter, cocoa, and milk in saucepan and bring to a boil. Continue boiling for 1 ½ minutes. Remove from heat and add oats, nuts, vanilla, and peanut butter. Beat until well blended. Spoon individual cookies onto waxed paper. [Note: can use smooth or crunchy peanut butter, as preferred.]

CHOCOLATE OATMEAL COOKIES

2 C SUGAR
½ C COCOA POWDER
½ C MILK
1 STICK BUTTER

½ C PEANUT BUTTER
1 TBSP VANILLA
3 C ROLLED OATS

Cook sugar, cocoa, milk, and butter for 1 minutes. Add peanut butter. Stir in vanilla and oatmeal. Mix and drop on waxed paper.

APPLESAUCE OATMEAL COOKIES

6 TBSP SOFT SHORTENING
½ C SUGAR
¼ C MOLASSES
1 EGG
¾ C FLOUR
½ TSP BAKING SODA

½ TSP CINNAMON
¾ C APPLESAUCE
½ CHOPPED NUTS
½ C RAISINS
1 ½ C ROLLED OATS
½ TSP SALT

Put shortening, sugar, molasses, and egg in deep bowl. Beat with spoon until thoroughly blended. Stir together flour, salt, soda, and cinnamon. Add to first mixture. Blend well. Stir in remaining ingredients. Drop on greased cookie sheet about 2 inches apart. Bake in moderate over, 375 degrees, about 12 minutes. Makes about 3 dozen.

HALLIE'S SUGAR COOKIES

¾ C SHORTENING + BUTTER (½ EACH)
1 ½ C SUGAR
2 EGGS
1 TSP SALT

1 TSP VANILLA
2 ½ C FLOUR
1 TSP BAKING PWDER
SUGAR FOR GARNISH

Mix together into dough and chill for 1 hour. Roll out to ½ inch thick. Cut and sprinkle with extra sugar. Bake until light brown, 8 to 10 minutes, at 400 degrees. Makes about 4 dozen.

Cakes, Cobblers & Crumbles

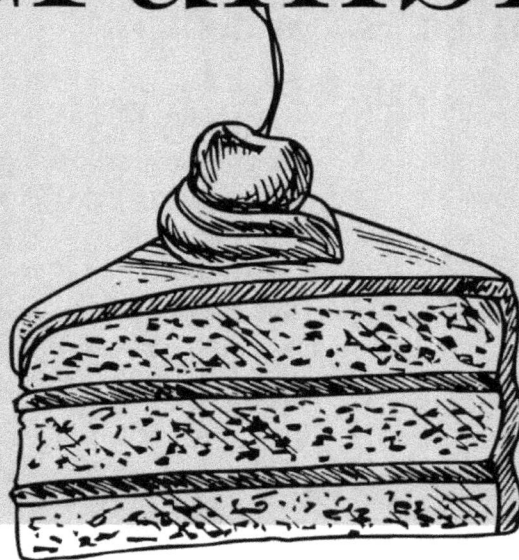

LAZY DAISY OATMEAL CAKE

1 ¼ C BOILING WATER
1 C OATS
½ C BUTTER
1 C GRANULATED SUGAR
1 C BROWN SUGAR
1 TSP VANILLA

2 EGGS
1 ½ C ALL PURPOSE FLOUR
1 TSP SODA
½ TSP SALT
¾ TSP CINNAMON
¼ TSP NUTMEG

Pour boiling water over oats, cover, and let stand 20 minutes. Beat butter until creamy. Add sugars and beat until fluffy. Blend in vanilla and eggs. Add oats to mixture; mix well. Sift together flour, soda, salt, cinnamon, and nutmeg. Add to creamed mixture. Mix well. Pour batter into well-greased and floured 9-inch square pans. Bake in preheated moderate over, 350 degrees, for 50 to 55 minutes. Do not remove cake from pan.

LAZY DAISY FROSTING

¼ C BUTTER, MELTED
½ C BROWN SUGAR
3 TBSP MILK OR HALF N HALF

1/3 C CHOPPED NUTS
¾ C COCONUT, DESSICATED

Combine all ingredients, boil until frosting becomes bubbly. Spread evenly over cake. Cake may be served warm or cold.

SWEET POTATO SURPRISE CAKE

1 ½ C COOKING OIL
2 C SUGAR
2 ½ C SIFTED CAKE FLOUR
3 TSP BAKING POWDER
¼ TSP SALT
1 TSP CINNAMON

4 EGGS
4 TBSP HOT WATER
1 TSP GROUND NUTMEG
1 ½ C GRATED SWEET POTATO
1 C CHOPPED NUTS
1 TSP VANILLA

Combine cooking oil and sugar and beat until smooth. Add egg yolks and beat well. Add hot water, then dry ingredients which have been sifted together. Stir in potatoes, nuts, and vanilla and beat well. Beat egg whites until stiff and fold into mixture. Bake in three greased 8 inch layer cake pans at 350 degrees for 25 to 30 minutes. Cool and frost.

SURPRISE CAKE FROSTING

1 LARGE CAN EVAPORATED MILK	3 EGG YOLKS
1 C SUGAR	1 TSP VANILLA
1 STICK MARGARINE	1 ½ C FLAKED COCONUT

Combine milk, sugar, margarine, egg yolks, and vanilla in saucepan. Cook over medium heat about 12 minutes, stirring constantly, until mixture thickens. Remove from heat and add coconut. Beat until cool and of spreading consistency.

CARROT CAKE

2 C SUGAR	4 EGGS
1 C WESSON OIL	3 C GRATED CARROTS
2 TSP CINNAMON	2 C FLOUR
1 TSP BAKING SODA	½ TSP SALT

Sift flour, salt, cinnamon, sugar, and soda together. Add eggs, oil, and carrots. Beat about 4 minutes on medium speed. Grease pans and sprinkle with flour. Bake at 350 degrees for 10 minutes. Turn over to 300 degrees and bake for 30 minutes. Frost.

CARROT CAKE FROSTING

1 BOX CONFECTIONERS SUGAR	8 OZ CREAM CHEESE
½ LB MARGARINE	1 TSP VANILLA
1 C CHOPPED NUTS	

Mix all ingredients and spread on cake.

QUICK CHOCOLATE CAKE

1 C SUGAR
3 TBSP COCOA POWDER
1 ½ C FLOUR
1 C COLD WATER
6 TBSP SHORTENING

1 TSP BAKING SODA
½ TSP SALT
1 TBSP VINEGAR
1 TSP VANILLA

Mix all ingredients until batter is smooth. Smooth into an 8x8x2 inch pan and bake for 20 to 25 minutes in 350 degree oven. Spread quick frosting on top.

QUICK CHOCOLATE FROSTING

1 C SUGAR
2 TBSP COCOA POWDER
¼ C BUTTER OR MARGARINE

¼ C MILK
1 TBSP LIGHT CORN SYRUP

Mix all ingredients. Bring to a full boil, cook for 2 minutes. Remove from heat. When lukewarm, beat until thick enough to spread over top of cake. Store in covered pan.

APPLESAUCE FRUIT CAKE

WET INGREDIENTS:
½ C BUTTER
1 ½ C SUGAR
1 C APPLESAUCE
½ TSP BAKING SODA

NUT INGREDIENTS:
2 C CHOPPED PECANS
1 C CHOPPED RAISINS
½ LB MIXED DRIED FRUIT

DRY INGREDIENTS:
2 ½ C FLOUR
1 TSP BAKING POWDER
½ TSP SALT
1 TSP CINNAMON
1 TSP ALLSPICE
½ TSP NUTMEG

Chop nuts, raisins, and fruit.

Cream butter and sugar. Add soda to applesauce. Set aside while mixing dry.

Sift together spices, add remaining dry ingredients. Add nuts and fruits. Add dry ingredients to creamed butter and sugar. Then add applesauce and soda mixture. Combine all together and pour into tube caked pan. Bake at 250 degrees for 2 ½ hours.

OLD FASHIONED POUND CAKE

½ LB BUTTER   ½ C SHORTENING
3 C SUGAR   6 EGGS
3 C FLOUR   ½ TSP BAKING POWDER
½ TSP SALT   1 TSP VANILLA
1 C MILK

Cream butter and shortening together. Mix in sugar and eggs and beat until incorporated. Add flour, baking powder, salt, vanilla, and milk. Beat until batter is light and creamy. Pour into well-greased 10 inch tube pan. Bake for 1 hour and 20 minutes at 325 degrees. Turn upside on wire rack and let cool.

GLAMOUR TORTE

1 PACKAGE CAKE MIX   14 OZ SWEETNED FLAKE COCONUT
1/2 C SUGAR   1 C NUTS
1 TBSP CORNSTARCH   ¾ C CHERRIES
¼ TSP SALT   1 TBSP CONFECTIONERS SUGAR
2 EGG YOLKS   ½ TSP VANILLA
1 CAN PINEAPPLE, CRUSHED   ½ PT CREAM

Make, bake, and cool cake as label directs. Meanwhile, in saucepan combine sugar, cornstarch, and salt. Add egg yolks. Mix well, stir in undrained pineapple and COCONUT. Cook over medium heat. Stir until thickened. Refrigerate. Cut cake into two layers, then split further into four layers. Stir nuts and cherries into cold pineapple/coconut mixture, and use as filling between layers. Whip cream, stir in confectioners' sugar and vanilla, and use to frost top of cake. Refrigerate several hours before serving.

CHERRY PUDDING CAKE

1 CAN CHERRY PIE FILLING   1 PACKAGE CAKE MIX
1 ½ C WATER   ½ STICK MARGARINE/BUTTER

Pour cherry pie filling into glass baking dish. Pour water on top of filling. Pour cake mix on top of water. Cut margarine/butter into 6 pieces and distribute on top of cake mix. Bake in 350 degree oven for 35 minutes.

RAISIN CAKE

1 BOX RAISINS
2 C WATER
¾ C LARD
2 C SUGAR
1 TSP MIXED SPICE

½ TSP SALT
1 C BOILED COFFEE, COOLED
1 TBSP BAKING SODA
FLOUR

Boil raisins in 2 cups of until water cooks out. Add lard, sugar, spices, salt, coffee, and baking soda dissolved in warm water. Add enough flour to mix a thick batter. Bake on 350 degrees for 30 - 40 minutes.

GUNGER CAKE

BLEND:
4/3 C SHORTENING
2 EGGS
1 C MOLASSES
1 C SUGAR

ADD:
1 TSP BAKING SODA
1 CUP BOILING WATER

SIFT TOGETHER:
2 C FLOUR
1 ½ TSP SALT
1 TSP CINNAMON
1 TSP DRIED GINGER
¼ TSP NUTMEG
½ ALLSPICE

BLEND and then mix in SIFTED together ingredients. Mix together well then ADD soda and boiling water. Beat well, add to greased pan, and bake at 400 degrees for 20 to 25 minutes.

LEMON SUPREME SPECIAL

1 PKG LEMON SUPREME CAKE MIX
½ C SUGAR
½ C SUGAR

4 EGGS
1 C APRICOT NECTAR
½ VEGETABLE OIL

Blend all ingredients in a large bowl, then beat at medium speed for 2 minutes. Spread batter in a greased and floured 10 inch pan. Bake at 350 for 45 to 55 minutes, until center springs back when lightly touched. Cool in pan for 15 minutes. Glaze: Blend 1 C confectioners' and 2 TBSP lemon juice. Pour over cake while warm.

APPLESAUCE CAKE

2 C SUGAR
3 EGGS
1 C BUTTER
2 C APPLESAUCE
1 C STRAWBERRY PRESERVES
1 C PINEAPPLE PRESERVES
1 LB PECANS OR WALNUTS

1 SMALL BOTTLE CHERRIES
1 LB RAISINS
1 TSP BAKING SODA
1 TSP NUTMEG
1 TSP CINNAMON
3 C PLAIN FLOUR

Mix eggs, butter, and sugar and cream together. Add applesauce, preserves, and cherries. Mix flour, nuts, raisins, and other dry ingredients together and add it mixture. Place whole cherries and pecans on top of cake batter. Bake in tube pan lined with waxed paper 2 ½ or 3 hours at 300 degrees.

FRUIT COCKTAIL CAKE

2 C FLOUR
2 C SUGAR
2 EGGS

1 TSP BAKING SODA
½ TSP SALT
1 LB CAN FRUIT COCKTAIL

FOR FROSTING:
¼ LB MARGARINE/BUTTER
1 C SUGAR
½ C PECANS, CHOPPED

2/3 C MILK
1 C SHREDDED COCONUT

Mix all ingredients together in a bowl. Put the mixture into an ungreased 13x9x2 inch pan. Bake at 350 degrees until cake is done. Pour frosting over cake while cake and frosting are both hot. After cooling, cut into squares.

To make frosting: Combine all ingredients in a pan and heat but do not boil.

PINEAPPLE ICE BOX CAKE

1 LB VANILLA WAFERS
½ C BUTTER
2 EGGS

1 ½ C POWDERED SUGAR
1 PT CREAM
1 CAN CRUSHED PINEAPPLE, DRAINED

Roll vanilla wafers into fine crumbs and divide into three equal parts. Put 1/3 of crumbs in bottom of square dish. Beat together the butter, eggs, and powdered sugar until creamy. Pour over crumb layer. Add another layer of crumbs. Whip cream until stiff and fold in pineapple. Pour over 2nd ^{cr}umb layer. Put remaining crumbs on top. Best if chilled in refrigerator overnight.

TUNNEL OF FUDGE CAKE

1 ½ C SOFT BUTTER
6 EGGS
1 ½ C SUGAR

2 PKG FUDGE FROSTING MIX
2 C CHOPPED NUTS
2 C REGULAR FLOUR

FOR THE GLAZE:
¾ C CONFECTIONERS' SUGAR
4 TO 6 TEASPOONS MILK

¼ C COCOA POWDER

Cream butter in large bowl at high speed with sugar and eggs. By hand, stir in flour, frosting mix, and nuts. Bake at 350 degrees for 1 hour in greased Bundt pan. Let cake cool in pan for 2 hours before removing. Drizzle the glaze over cooled cake. Let sit 20 minutes for glaze to set.

To make glaze: Whisk confectioners' sugar, cocoa powder, and milk. Start with small amount of milk and add more if needed.

PEACH COBBLER

¼ LB BUTTER OR MARAGAINE
¾ C FLOUR
1 C SUGAR
¼ TSP CINNAMON

½ TSP BAKING POWDER
½ C MILK
1 LARGE CAN PEACHES WITH SYRUP

Melt butter in baking pan. Mix dry ingredients and pour in pan with butter. Heat peaches and pour in baking pan over butter mixture. Sprinkle with ¼ tsp cinnamon and bake at 375 degrees for 30 to 35 minutes.

GRAHAM CRACKER CAKE

½ LB MARGARINE OR BUTTER
2 C SUGAR
5 EGGS
2 TSP VANILLA
1 C MILK
FOR FROSTING:
1 LARGE CAN CRUSHED PINEAPPLE
¼ LB MARAGRINE OR BUTTER

1 C SHREDDED COCONUT
1 C WALNUTS
2 TSP BAKING POWDER
1 LARGE BOX GRAHAM CRACKERS

1 BOX CONFECTIONERS SUGAR

Mix together, adding eggs one at a time, and put into 3 layer pans. Bake at 325 degrees until done. To make frosting drain pineapple and spread over layers. Miss margarine, sugar, and use pineapple juice to thin until desired consistency. Spread over pineapple topping. Combine layers.

WHITE FRUITCAKE

1 C SHREDDED COCONUT
1 C DICED CANDIED CITRON
1 C SEEDLESS RAISINS
1 C CURRANTS
1 C CHOPPED CANDIED PINEAPPLE
1 C CANDIED CHERRIES
2 C BLANCHED ALMONDS, CHOPPED

2 C BLANCHED PECANS, CHOPPED
3 C SIFTED FLOUR
1 C SHORTENING
2 C SUGAR
1 ½ TSP VANILLA
8 EGG WHITES
1 C FRUITS SYRUP

Combine first six ingredients with 1 cup flour. Sift remaining flour with baking powder. Cream shortening with sugar and flavouring until fluffy. Add sifted dry ingredients and fruit syrup alternately in small amounts beating well after each addition. Add fruit mixture. Beat egg whites until stiff but not dry and fold into batter. Pour into greased pans lined with greased parchment paper and bake in very slow oven at 275 degrees for about 4 hours. Makes 5 lb fruitcake.

QUICK APPLE CRUMBLE

1 CAN APPLE PIE FILLING
1 TBSP LEMON JUICE
1/3 C PLAIN FLOUR
1 C QUICK COOKING OATS

½ C BROWN SUGAR
½ TSP SALT
1 TSP CINNAMON
1/3 C MELTED BUTTER OR MARGARINE

Place apples in baking dish. Combine dry ingredients. Add butter and mix until crumble. Sprinkle over apples. Bake at 375 degrees for 30 minutes. Serve with ice cream or whipped cream.

OLD FASHIONED APPLE CRUMBLE

6 MEDIUM APPLES
½ C WHITE SUGAR
1 TSP CINNAMON
¾ C WATER
1/S TSP SALT

6 TSP BUTTER
½ C BROWN SUGAR
1 C SIFTED FLOUR
1 TSP BAKING POWDER

Peel apples and cut into slice. Place in saucepan with white sugar, cinnamon, water and cook until apples are soft. Then place in 9 inch pan. Cream shortening, add brown sugar and cream together well. Sift flour and baking powder and add to brown sugar mixture and make crumble. Sprinkle over apples in pan. Bake about 45 minutes in 350 degree over.

TUNNEL OF FUDGE CAKE

1 ½ C SOFT BUTTER
6 EGGS
1 ½ C SUGAR

2 PKG FUDGE FROSTING MIX
2 C CHOPPED NUTS
2 C REGULAR FLOUR

FOR THE GLAZE:
¾ C CONFECTIONERS' SUGAR
4 TO 6 TEASPOONS MILK

¼ C COCOA POWDER

Cream butter in large bowl at high speed with sugar and eggs. By hand, stir in flour, frosting mix, and nuts. Bake at 350 degrees for 1 hour in greased Bundt pan. Let cake cool in pan for 2 hours before removing. Drizzle the glaze over cooled cake. Let sit 20 minutes for glaze to set.

To make glaze: Whisk confectioners' sugar, cocoa powder, and milk. Start with small amount of milk and add more if needed.

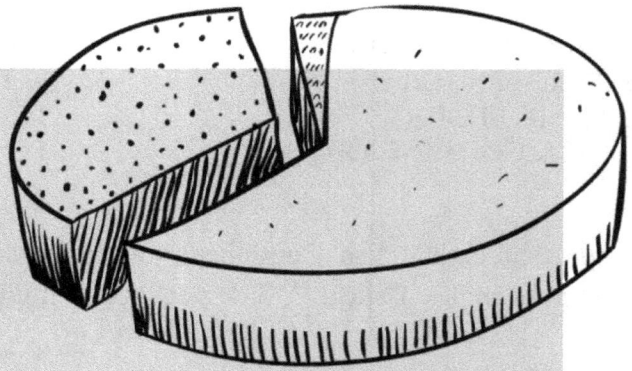

Pies,
Sweets
&
Sundries

OLD FASHIONED MERINGUE PIE TOPPING

5 LARGE EGG WHITES, ROOM TEMP   1/4 TSP CREAM OF TARTAR
1/4 C SUGAR

Beat egg whites and cream of tartar at high speed until foamy. Gradually add sugar, 1 TBSP at a time. Beat until stiff peaks form and sugar is dissolved.

Use for any pie calling for meringue topping.

QUICK COUNTRY PIE CRUST

1 1/3 C ALL-PURPOSE FLOUR   1/2 TSP SALT
½ C COLD SHORTENING   3 TO 6 TBSP ICE COLD WATER

Combine flour and salt until blended well. Cut shortening into flour mixture until about pea size crumbles. Add cold water, a little at a time, stirring with fork until dough just holds together and makes a ball. Chill at least 30 minutes before rolling out or shaping.

SWEET POTATO PIE

2 EGGS   1/8 TS NUTMEG
1 C SUGAR   1 TSP CINNAMON
1 TSP SALT   1 C MILK
2 TBSP BUTTER OR MARGARINE   1 ½ C MASHED SWEET POTATOES
1 UNBAKED PIE SHELL

Beat eggs slightly; add sugar, spices, and milk. Add butter or margarine to mashed sweet potatoes and blend with milk and egg mixture. Pour into unbaked pie shell and bake at 450 degrees for 10 minutes. Reduce heat to 350 and bake 30 to 40 minutes or until filling is firm.

CHOCOLATE PIE

3 TBSP COCOA POWDER
2 ½ C COLD MILK
1 C SUGAR
½ TSP SALT

3 EGGS YOLKS, BEATEN
2 TBSP BUTTER
2 TBSP VANILLA EXTRACT
4 TBSP FLOUR

Mix sugar, flour, cocoa, and salt. Add small amount of milk, mix in eggs yolks, then add remaining milk. Bring to a boil and stir constantly until mixture thickens. Remove from heat, add vanilla and pour into cooked pie shell. Top with meringue.

COCONUT PIE

½ C SUGAR
1/3 C FLOUR
¼ TSP SALT
2 C MILK

2 EGGS, SEPERATED
1 TSP VANILLA
14 OZ SWEETENED COCONUT FLAKES
¼ STICK MARGARINE OR BUTTER

Blend sugar, flour, salt together in large saucepan. Add ½ cup milk, stirring until smooth; add remaining milk and eggs. Cook until thick and remove from heat. Add butter and vanilla and coconut. Pour into large 9 inch prepared pie shell. Beat egg whites into meringue and cover pie.

HAWAIIAN BANANA PIE

6 C SLICED BANANAS, RIPE BUT FIRM
¾ C PINEAPPLE JUICE
¾ C PINEAPPLE JUICE
¾ C SUGAR

1 TBSP FLOUR
1 ½ TSP CINNAMON
1 TBSP BUTTER
PIE CRUST, TOP AND BOTTOM

Soak bananas in pineapple juice 20 to 30 minutes. Drain but save juice. Heat oven to 400 degrees. Place bananas in pastry lined pie pan. Blend sugar, flour, and cinnamon and sprinkle over bananas. Add 3 TBSP of the pineapple juice, dot with butter and cover with top crust which has slits cut into it. Seal and flute. Bake 30 to 45 minutes or until crust is browned.

BRIGHT COCONUT PIE

½ C SUGAR
1/3 C FLOUR
PINCH OF SALT
2 C MILK
3 EGG YOLKS

1 TSP VANILLA
½ TSP LEMON JUICE
1 TBSP BUTTER
14 OZ SHREDDED COCONUT

In saucepan, combine sugar, flour, and salt. Beat egg yolks, add about ¼ c of milk to the yolks. Beat well, then mix with remaining milk into the dry ingredients. Cook over medium heat until mixture thickens. Remove from heat, add vanilla, lemon, butter, and coconut. Mix well, pour into baked pie crust. Cover with meringue. Brown in oven. Cool and serve.

PINEAPPLE PIE

1 LARGE CAN CRUSHED PINEAPPLE
1 LARG CAN EVAPORATED MILK
6 EGGS

1 STICK BUTTER
2 C SUGAR
2 TBSP FLOUR

Beat egg yolks, add sugar and flour. Stir in melted butter, milk, and pineapple. Cook in saucepan stirring constantly until thick. Pour into baked shell. Cover with meringue. Bake at 425 degrees for 40 minutes or until knife comes clean in center.

CHERRY CREAM CHEESE PIE

1 BAKED PASTRY SHELL, 9 INCH
8 OZ CREAM CHEESE
1 TSP VANILLA

15.5 OZ CONDENSED MILK
1/3 C LEMON JUICE
1 CAN CHERRY PIE FILLING

Soften cream cheese to room temperature. Whip until fluffy. Gradually add condensed milk. Continue to beat well until blended. Add lemon juice and vanilla. Blend well. Pour into crust. Chill 2 hours and then garnish with cherry pie filling on top. Chill for an additional hour.

QUICK STRAWBERRY PIE

1 C SELF RISING FLOUR
1 C SUGAR + ½ C SUGAR
1 C MILK

¾ STICK MARGARINE (OR BUTTER)
2 C STRAWBERRIES

Melt margarine/butter in pan. Mix flour, sugar, and milk, then pour in center of pan over melted margarine/butter. Pour the strawberries in the center of pan. Do not stir. Sprinkle an additional ½ C sugar over pie. Bake at 375 degrees for 30 to 35 minutes.

OLD FASHIONED LEMON PIE

2 C WATER
4 EGG YOLKS
1 C SUGAR
¼ TSP SALT

½ C LEMON JUICE
5 TBSP CORNSTARCH
8 INCH PIE SHELL, BAKED

Mix cornstarch, sugar, salt, and water. Bring to a boil in the top of a double boiler. Cool until thickened and smooth. Stir often. Requires about 20 minutes to thicken. Beat egg yolks, blend with a little of the warm cornstarch mixture, add all egg to cornstarch once tempered. Put back on double boiler and cook for 5 minutes, stirring constantly. Remove from heat. Add lemon juice. It should be thick enough to hold its shape. Cool slightly before pouring into cooled baked shell. Top with meringue.

CHOCOLATE PECAN FUDGE

2 OZ UNSWEETENED BAKERS CHOCOLATE
¾ C MILK
2 C SUGAR
1 C CHOPPED PECANS

DASH OF SALT

2 TBSP BUTTER
1 TSP VANILLA

Place chocolate and milk in heavy saucepan. Cook and stir over very low heat until blended. Add sugar and salt, stir over medium heat to a boil. Continue boiling without stirring until a little forms a soft ball in cold (temp of 324 degrees). Remove from heat. Add butter and vanilla and pecans. Cool to lukewarm. Beat until mixture holds shaped and is glossy, and then smooth into large pan. Cut when cool.

NEVER FAIL FUDGE

3 C SUGAR
½ C COCOA POWDER
4 TBSP CORN SYRUP
12 OZ EVAPORATED MILK

3 TBSP BUTTER
1 TSP VANILLA
NUTS

Combine sugar, cocoa, and salt. Add corn syrup and milk. Cook to soft ball stage, 232 degrees. Remove from heat and add butter. Let stand without stirring until cool. Add vanilla and beat until thick. Spread into pan and cool to cut.

CINNAMON COATED PECANS

1 C SUGAR
½ TSP CINNAMON
1 TSP VANILLA

¼ C EVAPORATED MILK
2 TBSP WATER
2 C PECAN HALVES

Cook first four ingredients over medium heat until mixture will form a soft ball in cold water. Add vanilla. Pour pecans into mixture and coat well. Spread onto waxed paper and let cool.

FRUIT SALAD

2 EGGS BEATEN
3 TBSP VINEGAR
2 C FRUIT SALAD
2 C CRUSHED PINEAPPLE

4 TBSP SUGAR
3 TBSP BUTTER
2 C MARSHMALLOWS
1 C CREAM

Put beaten eggs in double boiler. Add vinegar and sugar. Cook until mixture coats spoon. Remove from boiler and add butter. Cool. Whip 1 cup of cream. Add to mixture of fruit and marshmallows. Chill several hours.

LIME MARSHMALLOW SALAD

1 PCKG LIME JELLO
1 C BOILING WATER
1 SMALL CAN CRUSHED PINEAPPLE
2 TSP LEMON JUICE
16 OZ CREAM CHEESE

PINCH OF SALT
¼ C SUGAR
1 C SMALL MARSHMALLOWS
1 C CHOPPED PECANS
½ C WHIPPING CREAM

Combine Jello, hot water, sugar, and lemon juice. Cool and add all other ingredients. Fold in whipped cream. Place in refrigerator to chill.

RUSSIAN SALAD

8 OZ CREAM CHEESE
1 PKG LIME JELLO
1 C HOT WATER
15 SMALL MARHSMALLOWS
8 OZ CAN CRUSHED PINEAPPLE

1/3 C MAYONNAISE
¾ C MILK
½ C NUTS
½ C BANANAS

Melt cream cheese and marshmallows together over low heat. Dissolve Jello with hot water and add to cheese mixture. Cool. Add mayonnaise, milk, nuts, bananas, and pineapple when cool. Chill until set.

FROZEN FRUIT SALAD

½ PAKG MINI MARSHMALLOWS

2 BANANAS, CUT FINE
20 OZ CAN FRUIT COCKTAIL

6 OZ SOUR CREAM OR WHIPPED TOPPING
1 C FRESH OR FROZEN STRAWBERRIES

Drain fruit cocktail. Mix all ingredients together and freeze. Thaw slightly before serving.

FLUFFY FLUFFY FROSTING

1 LB CONFECTIONERS SUGAR
1 EGG WHITE
¼ LB MARGARINE

DASH OF SALT
1 TSP VANILLA OR LEMON EXTRACT
2 OR 3 TBSP CORN SYRUP

Beat egg white and dash of salt until fluffy. Sift sugar and add small amount at a time to egg white. (This cooks the white so it doesn't run) Add corn syrup, margarine, extract, and remaining sugar alternately. If frosting is too stiff, add small amount of milk until smooth enough for spreading. Continue beating at medium speed until fluffy.

COCOA MOCHA FROSTING

6 TBSP COLD COFFEE
1 LB CONFECTIONERS SUGAR
½ TSP SAL

1 TSP VANILLA
1 CUP COCOA, SIFTED
6 TBSP BUTTER, SOFTENED

Combine coffee and vanilla. Sift together sugar, cocoa, and salt. Add to liquid in 3 parts, beating well. Gradually beat in softened butter, in parts, until creamy and smooth. Covers about 18 petit fours.

LEMON CUSTARD SAUCE FOR POUND CAKES

1 C COLD MILK
¾ C LIGHT CORN SYRUP
1 PKG INSTANT LEMON PUDDING

½ C CHOPPED PECANS
2 TSP FRESH LEMON JUICE

Beat milk, syrup, and pudding mix until smooth. Add pecans and lemon juice. Beat again. Serve over slices of pound cake.

COOKED FRUIT DRESSING

¼ C SUGAR
1 ½ TBSP FLOUR
1 WHOLE EGG

1 LEMON, JUICED
½ C PINEAPPLE JUICE
½ C HEAVY CREAM, WHIPPED

Combine sugar, flour, and egg. Add fruit juices. Cook on top of double boiler until thick. Cool and fold into whipped cream. Serve over fruit salads or pound cake.

CITRUS WEDDING PUNCH

1 C WATER
1 C SUGAR
9 C ORANGE JUICE

3 C GRAPEFRUIT JUICE
1 C LIME JUICE
1 LITER GINGER ALE

Combine sugar and water in saucepan. Place over heat and stir until sugar is dissolved. Bring to a boil. Let boil 5 minutes without stirring. Cool. Add grapefruit, orange, and lime juices. Just before serving, add ginger ale. Makes 36 punch cup servings.

MABEL'S KOOL AID PUNCH

4 PACKETS STRAWBERRY KOOL AID
4 LARGE CANS PINEAPPLE JUICE
2 ½ LITERS ORNGE JUICE
3 JARS CHERRIES, DRAINED

3 QTS WATER
3 CANS CRUSHED PINEAPPLE
5 LBS SUGAR

Mix all together. Add ice just before serving. Makes 5 gallons or enough for 50 people.

Notes & Extra Recipes_____

Notes & Extra Recipes

MOODY BOXFAN
BOOKS

www.ingramcontent.com/pod-product-compliance
Lightning Source LLC
LaVergne TN
LVHW081400060426
835510LV00016B/1923